Nature's Changes

CHANGING SEASONS

Bobbie Kalman & Kelley MacAulay

🌳 Crabtree Publishing Company

www.crabtreebooks.com

Created by Bobbie Kalman

Dedicated by Margaret Amy Salter
For my Grandpa, William Reiach—a man in winter plumage with spring in his heart.

Editor-in-Chief
Bobbie Kalman

Writing team
Bobbie Kalman
Kelley MacAulay

Substantive editor
Kathryn Smithyman

Editors
Molly Aloian
Robin Johnson
Reagan Miller
Rebecca Sjonger

Design
Margaret Amy Salter
Samantha Crabtree (cover)
Robert MacGregor (series logo)

Print and production coordinator
Katherine Berti

Photo research
Crystal Sikkens

Consultant
Patricia Loesche, Ph.D., Animal Behavior Program,
Department of Psychology, University of Washington

Special thanks to
Sophie Izikson

Illustrations
Barbara Bedell: pages 7 (top), 11, 18, 28, 30 (holly)
Antoinette "Cookie" Bortolon: page 30 (pine cones)
© Crabtree Publishing Company: pages 6, 7 (bottom-left and right)
Katherine Berti: pages 8, 9, 31
Margaret Amy Salter: series logo illustrations, pages 15, 21, 24,
     30 (butterfly)
Bonna Rouse: pages 22, 30 (flowers and seed)

Photographs
Bobbie Kalman: page 19 (bottom left)
Visuals Unlimited: Steve Maslowski: page 28
Other images by Adobe Image Library, Comstock, Corbis,
     Corel, Creatas, Digital Stock, Digital Vision, Eyewire,
     Otto Rogge Photography, and Photodisc

Crabtree Publishing Company

www.crabtreebooks.com   1-800-387-7650

Printed in the U.S.A./012013/SN20130104.

Library of Congress Cataloging-in-Publication Data
Kalman, Bobbie.
   Changing seasons / Bobbie Kalman and Kelley MacAulay.
     p. cm. -- (Nature's changes series)
   Includes index.
   ISBN-13: 978-0-7787-2275-5 (RLB)
   ISBN-10: 0-7787-2275-9 (RLB)
   ISBN-13: 978-0-7787-2309-7 (pbk.)
   ISBN-10: 0-7787-2309-7 (pbk.)
   1. Phenology--Juvenile literature. 2. Seasons--Juvenile literature.
   I. MacAulay, Kelley. II. Title.
   QH544.K35 2005
   578.4'2--dc22
                                                    2005000492
                                                    LC

Published in Canada
Crabtree Publishing
616 Welland Ave.
St. Catharines, Ontario
L2M 5V6

Published in the United States
Crabtree Publishing
PMB 59051
350 Fifth Avenue, 59th Floor
New York, New York 10118

Published in the United Kingdom
Crabtree Publishing
Maritime House
Basin Road North, Hove
BN41 1WR

Published in Australia
Crabtree Publishing
3 Charles Street
Coburg North
VIC 3058

Contents

The Earth

The Earth is divided into two halves by the **equator**. The equator is an imaginary line that runs around the middle of the Earth.

Up north

The top half of the Earth is called the **Northern Hemisphere**. It stretches from the equator to the **North Pole**. The North Pole is the area at the most northern part of the Earth.

Down south

The bottom half of the Earth is called the **Southern Hemisphere**. It stretches from the equator to the **South Pole**. The South Pole is the area at the most southern part of the Earth.

North Pole

NORTHERN HEMISPHERE

equator

SOUTHERN HEMISPHERE

South Pole

Many kinds of seals live
near the cold North Pole.

Always the same
In some parts of the Earth, the **climate** is always the same. Near the equator, it is hot year round. As you travel away from the equator, the temperatures get colder. At the North Pole and the South Pole, the weather is always cold.

Tigers live near the hot equator.

Penguins live near the cold South Pole.

5

Four seasons

In the areas between the equator and the poles, the temperatures are not the same year round. These areas of the Northern and Southern hemispheres have four **seasons** each year. A season is a period of time that has certain weather and temperatures. The four seasons are spring, summer, autumn or fall, and winter.

Spring is warm and is often rainy.

Summer is hot and sunny.

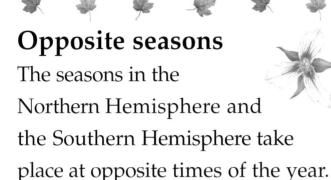

Opposite seasons

The seasons in the Northern Hemisphere and the Southern Hemisphere take place at opposite times of the year.

When it is summer in the Northern Hemisphere, it is winter in the Southern Hemisphere. This book is about seasons in the Northern Hemisphere.

Autumn is cool and windy. Leaves change color.

Winter is cold and snowy.

The tilted planet

Each year, the Earth circles once around the sun. It takes 365 days for the Earth to complete the circle. The Earth is tilted as it moves. For part of the year, the Northern Hemisphere is tilted toward the sun. During another part of the year, the Northern Hemisphere is tilted away from the sun. The tilt of the Earth causes the seasons to change throughout the year.

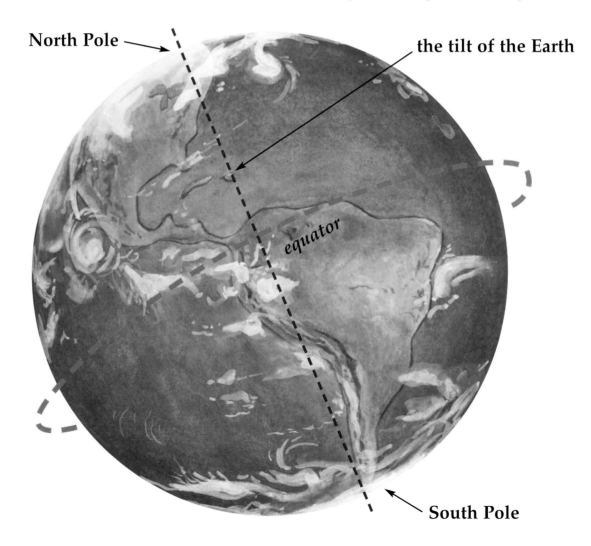

North Pole

the tilt of the Earth

equator

South Pole

Summer sunlight

When the North Pole is tilted toward the sun, the Northern Hemisphere receives a lot of sunlight. Plenty of sunlight causes summer.

Winter darkness

When the North Pole is tilted away from the sun, the Northern Hemisphere does not receive much sunlight. Little sunlight causes winter.

In autumn, the North Pole begins to tilt away from the sun.

In winter, the North Pole is tilted away from the sun.

SUN

In summer, the North Pole is tilted toward the sun.

In spring, the North Pole begins to tilt toward the sun.

Spring is here!

flower bud

Spring begins around March 21. The days are warm and often rainy. Buds appear on the stems or branches of plants. Before long, the buds will bloom into flowers. **Sap** starts to flow in the trees. Sap is a sweet liquid in plants. Maple sap, for example, is used to make maple syrup.

This fawn is tasting some new spring flowers.

Sprouting plants

As the soil warms up, seeds begin to **sprout** in the ground. The seeds send roots into the soil to find water. **Shoots** soon grow above the ground. Shoots are young plants. Sunlight and rain help leaves grow on the shoots. Soon, the plants will start making food.

A growing plant

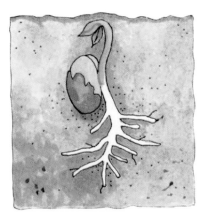

A seed sends out roots to find water in the soil.

In spring, many people plant gardens around their homes. Spring is also the time when farmers plant crops in their fields.

Shoots soon appear above the ground. The leaves on the shoots are bright green.

11

Springing to life!

The spring season is full of life! Hungry animals wake up from their winter sleep and search for food. The birds and animals that left for winter return to their summer homes. Animals **shed**, or lose their fur. The Pere David deer shown left is shedding its winter fur.

Hatching from eggs

Many birds lay eggs in spring. Baby birds **hatch** from the eggs. To hatch means to break out of an egg. Baby birds are hungry after they hatch! The parents gather food to feed their babies.

This mother bird has gathered food to feed to her babies.

New lives

Spring is the season when most animals have babies. To stay alive, baby animals need warm weather. They also need plenty of food to eat. In spring, the babies spend time playing and exploring. There are many new things to see!

This baby fox is sniffing a spring flower.

The mother cougar is cleaning her baby's fur.

Growing in summer

Summer begins around June 21.
Summer days are long and sunny.
Plants grow and spread their seeds.
They are in **full bloom**. The flowers
of plants in full bloom are fully grown.
Fruits and berries are also fully grown.
They are ready to be eaten.

This dandelion is covered with seeds. The seeds will blow away. New dandelions will grow where the seeds have landed.

*Insects are everywhere in summer! This butterfly is eating **nectar**. Nectar is a sweet liquid found in flowers.*

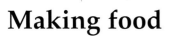

Making food

Summer days are hot and sunny. Heat and sunlight cause the leaves of plants to turn green. When the leaves are green, plants can use sunlight to make food. Making food using sunlight is called **photosynthesis**. Plants use the food they make to grow and to stay healthy.

Photosynthesis

Leaves contain a green **pigment**, or color, called **chlorophyll**. Chlorophyll takes in sunlight and uses it to make food for the plant.

Plants use sunlight to make food from air and water.

Animals such as young foxes often hide among summer plants.

Active animals

Animals are active in summer. There is plenty of food for them to eat. **Herbivores** are animals that eat plants. They spend summer days searching for plants and berries to eat. The porcupine on the left is eating summer flowers. **Carnivores** are animals that eat other animals. They spend their days hunting animals to eat.

Growing up

Baby animals grow quickly during the warm summer months. They watch their parents to learn how to find food. By the end of summer, most young animals will leave their parents and live on their own.

Beautiful birds

Summer is a great time for watching birds!
If you look up in the sky in the morning,
you may see a bald eagle. It may be
searching for fish or other animals
to eat. You may also see a cardinal
in your back yard. You can watch
as it flutters about looking
for seeds and insects to eat.
What color are cardinals?

bald eagle

*Male cardinals
are bright red, but
female cardinals are
much less colorful.*

*What do you enjoy doing in summer?
Many children love to go swimming!*

Autumn changes

A leaf is green in summer because it contains chlorophyll.

Autumn begins around September 22. In autumn, many changes take place in nature. The days become shorter and colder. It often rains. Leaves change color and fall to the ground. **Frost** appears on the ground and on the trees each morning. The leaf on the right is covered in frost.

In autumn, a leaf stops making food. The green color in the leaf fades. New colors in the leaf begin to show.

Before long, the leaf completely changes color.

Without its green color, the leaf cannot make food. It dries up and falls to the ground.

Autumn leaves can be red, orange, yellow, or purple.

New soil

Leaves cover the ground in autumn. As rain falls on the leaves, the leaves break into small pieces. Over time, the small pieces of leaves change into soil. In spring, new plants will grow in the soil. Many animals will feed on these new plants. The herbivores will eat the plants, and carnivores, such as this bobcat, will eat the herbivores.

Autumn harvest

Farmers **harvest** many kinds of food **crops** in autumn. To harvest is to gather crops from the fields where they grow. Farmers gather foods such as corn and wheat. Many people enjoy autumn activities such as apple picking.

Winter is coming!

In autumn, days become shorter and colder. Animals know that winter is coming. Some animals **migrate** south to areas where the winters are warm. To migrate means to move to a new place for a certain period of time.

Flying to winter homes

Most birds migrate south for winter. Some fly long distances. They go to the same places every year. Many kinds of birds travel in groups called **flocks**. The geese shown above are part of a large flock. Red-winged blackbirds, shown left, also migrate in groups.

On their way

Many insects die when the temperature turns cool in autumn. A few types of insects migrate south, however. Monarch butterflies, such as the one shown right, spend summer throughout Canada and the United States. In autumn, they fly to California and Mexico, where they spend winter.

*Some animals that migrate do not live on land! Humpback whales spend summer swimming in waters near Alaska. In autumn, they migrate south to warmer waters near Hawaii to have **calves**, or babies.*

Ready for winter

Most animals do not migrate. They spend autumn preparing for winter. Many animals find **dens**, or shelters, where they can keep warm in winter. When the animals have found dens, they get busy gathering food. They store the food in their dens for the cold days ahead.

This wood rat has made a den in a fallen log.

A long winter nap

Some animals **hibernate** in winter. To hibernate means to sleep through winter. When an animal hibernates, its heartbeat slows down. A slower heartbeat helps the animal save energy.

Some birds hibernate. This poorwill is hibernating in its den.

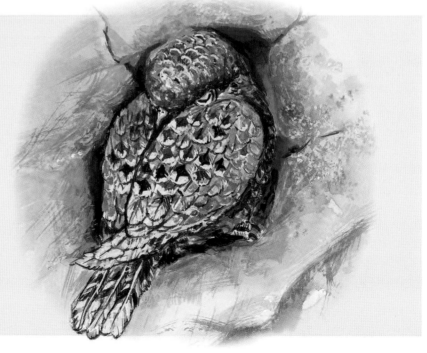

Adding layers

In autumn, animals eat a lot of food! The food adds fat to their bodies. The fat keeps the animals warm during winter. Most animals also grow thick layers of warm fur.

This red fox has grown a thick fur coat. The warm fur will protect the fox's body from the cold.

In autumn, a mother bear teaches her young how to fish for salmon. The young bears will eat a lot of salmon every day to add fat to their bodies. The bears will also eat berries and other plants.

White winter

Winter begins around December 22. It is the coldest season of the year. The days are short and dark. In some places, the ground and trees are covered with snow and ice. Freezing winds blow across the land.

A lynx has large paws that stop it from sinking too deeply into the winter snow.

Plants stop growing

In winter, the soil is frozen. During this time, most plants and trees are **dormant**. Dormant plants do not grow. They may look dead, but below the ground their roots are alive and healthy. The plants will not start growing again until the weather warms up in spring.

*Most trees lose their leaves in winter, but **conifers** do not. The leaves of conifers remain green all winter.*

Winter may be cold, but it is still a fun time of year! Many people go sledding or skiing down snow-covered hills. Other people enjoy ice-skating.

Staying alive

*Did you know that animals **shiver** to keep warm? When animals shiver, their bodies shake. Many animals, such as this seal, shiver when they lie down to sleep.*

You will not see many animals in winter! Most animals stay inside their warm dens. Some animals are hard to see because their fur has turned white. White fur blends in with snow. Carnivores find it harder to hunt animals that are hidden by their colors.

The fur of some rabbits turns white in winter. Having white fur helps the rabbits hide in snow.

In summer, the fur of some rabbits turns brown. Brown fur blends in with dirt and brown plants and hides the rabbits.

Where is the food?

Food is hard to find in winter. Plants are buried under snow. Many animals are hibernating, so carnivores have trouble finding animals to eat. In winter, most animals must travel long distances to look for food.

Wolves are carnivores. To find food, this wolf is sniffing for animals that are hibernating beneath the snow.

Woodpeckers do not migrate. In winter, they pull insects from the bark of trees.

Through the seasons

A great way to learn about the changing seasons is to watch one kind of animal throughout the year. Write down how that animal grows and changes as the seasons change. Squirrels are a good animal to study because they probably live close to your home!

In spring, baby squirrels are born in nests made by their mothers. Before long, the babies are ready to explore! These baby squirrels are taking their first look at the world outside their nest.

In summer, the active young squirrels run and play in the trees and grass. They eat many summer foods such as seeds, flowers, and berries.

The time for play is over when autumn arrives! Squirrels must gather foods to store for winter. They may gather acorns, nuts, and mushrooms.

You will have to watch carefully to see squirrels in winter! Many stay inside their warm nests. They sometimes go outside to gather foods, however, when it is sunny.

Sun catchers

It is exciting to watch the seasons change! A fun way to welcome the seasons is to hang a sun catcher in your window for each one. A sun catcher is a colorful piece of artwork that allows light to shine through. Look at the next page to learn how to make a sun catcher for each season.

Make a list

To begin, make a list of the colors and shapes you see in each season. For summer, you might choose the yellow sun, green plants, and red cardinals. Which colors and shapes might you see in the other seasons?

Make your sun catchers

1. Draw a shape onto a piece of waxed paper. Then trace the shape onto another piece of waxed paper.

2. Sharpen some old crayons in a crayon sharpener. Choose different colors for each season!

3. Place the crayon shavings between the two sheets of waxed paper. You can mix the colors together or use different colors for different parts of your shape.

4. Ask an adult to iron the waxed paper until the crayon shavings have melted.

5. Cut out your shape. Use some string to hang your sun catcher in a window. Hang a new sun catcher to celebrate each new season!

These sun catchers were made by mixing several colors together.

This sun catcher was made by putting different colors in different parts of the picture.

Words to know

Note: Boldfaced words that are defined in the text may not appear in the glossary.

carnivore An animal that eats other animals

climate The usual temperature and weather in a particular place

conifer A tree with cones and with leaves shaped like needles

crops Plants that are grown by people to be eaten as food

frost A thin layer of ice

herbivore An animal that eats mainly plant foods

hibernate To sleep through winter

migrate To move from one area to another place for a certain period of time such as for winter

photosynthesis The process by which green plants make food using sunlight, air, and water

shed To lose winter fur

sprout To begin growing roots, shoots, and buds

Index